Autism from the Inside
A Neurodiversity Action Guide for Employers

Autism *from the* Inside

A Neurodiversity Action Guide for Employers

by Melva Radtke

Published by RadtkeResources
Graphic design by Colleen Carlson
Layout by David Radtke
Edited by Bill Hammond
Image credits:
Cover image: iStock.com/orsonsurf
Traffic image: iStock.com/XXLPhoto
Traffic jam: by Rgoogin at the English Wikipedia, CC BY-SA 3.0, https://commons.wikimedia.org/w/index.php?curid=8931241

ISBN: 978-0-9885034-6-5 (e-book)

www.radtkeresources.com

Contents

The Neurodiversity Advantage

Diversity, equity, inclusion, and accessibility (DEIA) is good for business. It's not designed to prioritize one group over another. It's a strategy that fosters innovation in companies both large and small.

For large and mid-sized companies, it's a smart business practice that widens the pool of candidates available for open job positions. It has a strong correlation to higher employee satisfaction and productivity. And given the high prevalence of neurodivergent people, large employers already have neurodiverse employees on their payroll, whether they know it or not.

For small and micro companies, DEIA contributes to a positive reputation in the community which can translate to improved sales from word-of-mouth marketing. Small companies can build and sustain inclusive cultures swiftly and realize their benefits more quickly than larger companies. These are critical advantages for companies with limited budgets for publicizing their goods or services.

The focus of this Guide is neurodiversity, which is an important but sometimes overlooked dimension of diversity. As a general concept, neurodiversity celebrates the idea that each person's brain works differently and these differences are assets rather than deficits. It rejects the notion that everyone in a thriving organization must think exactly alike.

In a narrower sense, neurodiversity refers to individuals who are neurodivergent, i.e. who have neurologically-based learning differences. The term originally referred most commonly to autism but has more recently expanded to include ADHD, dyslexia, Tourette's, synesthesia and other learning and developmental differences. While this Action Guide focuses on the learning differences in autism, many of the suggested action steps could also be useful when working with neurodiverse employees who aren't autistic, especially those with ADHD and Dyslexia.

Neurodivergent employees can improve a company's value because they approach tasks with a fresh perspective that allows them to identify issues that others may have missed. They are quick to recognize patterns, they have strong memories, they pay close attention to detail and can easily spot irregularities. They can offer fresh insights about how to solve problems.

Despite their skills, autistic individuals are commonly not included in the diversity conversation. This is likely a factor in their alarmingly high rate of unemployment.[1] They have a higher rate of unemployment -- and underemployment -- than the general population and other disability groups. Autistics represent an important but untapped resource. They're ready, willing and able to work, especially for companies that commit to understanding their unique strengths and their challenges.

---

1 Although employment rates vary by region and population characteristics, various studies estimate that only 15–23% of autistic individuals in the U.S. are employed (Bureau of Labor Statistics, 2025; Hickey et al., 2024)

Perspectives on Autism - Medical Model vs. Social Model

How people think about autism can affect their approach to working with neurodivergent individuals. There are two predominant models of thought on disability – a medical model and a social model. The medical model views autism as a health problem that requires diagnosis, treatment and a cure. The focus is on how to "fix" a neurodivergent individual so they act more neurotypical to better fit into an existing system. It focuses on what is "wrong" with the person, instead of what that person needs to perform assigned tasks. Company managers with this perspective might, for example, reject simple accommodation requests or require neurodivergent employees to work with therapists to "eliminate neurodivergent behaviors" as part of an employee improvement plan. One problem with this approach is that it fails to consider the fact that many challenges faced by neurodivergent employees isn't autism – it's the societal and workplace barriers that don't account for how they process information.

The social model, on the other hand, focuses on the fact that there are different ways of thinking that don't necessarily align with a one-size-fits-all system. It doesn't deny the reality of developmental impairments, but contends that neurological differences are not inherently disabling. It encourages a shift in perspective that emphasizes the importance of creating supportive and adaptable environments for different types of thinkers. Company leaders with this perspective manage neurodiverse employees by fostering a culture of inclusion, which might include flexible working hours, co-worker mentoring and the availability of private spaces for short periods of rest.

Training for True Inclusion

Building a successful neurodiversity program doesn't mean a company has to compromise on employee performance standards or make changes in employee job functions. What it does require is visible leadership, operational flexibility and employee training that is consistent and not just a one-time event.

Training should focus on teaching employees to clearly understand the "why" behind neurodivergent workplace behaviors. With that understanding in place, employees can identify and learn how to manage unexpected situations involving neurodiverse workers, turning challenges into opportunities for improving the performance of neurodiverse employees and leveraging their value to the company.

This type of training builds a culture of true inclusion that is honored and understood by all employees. It helps ensure the success of neurodivergent employees. It also sharpens the management and customer service skills - such as diplomatic problem solving - of neurotypical employees.

Neurodiversity is a Two-Way Street

The purpose of this guide is to advance the idea that reciprocal understanding between employers and their neurodiverse employees is a core value of successful neurodiversity programs. Research papers, journal articles and blogs cite the valuable but often underappreciated contribution of neurodiverse employees to the companies that hire them.

The other side of the equation is also important. As neurodiverse employees can improve a company's bottom line, the company in turn should take steps to improve its understanding of how neurodiverse employees think and learn – both as a matter of building excellence in management practices and to create a humane workplace where diverse perspectives are a valued aspect of the company culture.

Ask Why

Many of us observe how neurodivergent individuals behave in job situations and from that, draw general conclusions about their personalities, skills and work ethic. We see one side of them and apply it to the whole. If a neurodivergent employee doesn't complete an assigned task, we might assume it's because he's lazy when in truth, he may have been confused about what he was supposed to do and was afraid to ask for help. Or he may be taking frequent bathroom breaks – not to avoid work, but to find respite from workplace noises that trigger uncomfortable and distracting sensory responses.

Autism from the Inside explores the question of how neurodivergent individuals think and learn. It looks beyond their in-the-moment behaviors and asks why they respond in unexpected ways when asked to perform tasks or follow company rules. The aim is to help managers and co-workers handle unexpected (and sometimes unwanted) situations in a way that facilitates the success of neurodivergent employees while promoting the company's goals for success in the marketplace.

An important note: This isn't a psychology crash course. This is a guide for employers and neurodivergent employees that is based on the common-sense understanding that knowing the underpinnings of neurodivergent behavior can help employers effectively manage neurodivergent workers and build rapport among team members at all levels of skill and rank.

Definitions and Word Matters

Industry groups use terms of art to describe their organizational norms and practices. So, too, in the autism community, some words or phrases that seem ordinary and interchangeable are terms of art which convey nuanced meanings about what it's like to be neurodivergent. Being aware of the perceived meaning of different words in the autism community can help neurotypical individuals build rapport and communicate their intention to understand and respect the neurodivergent experience.

Neurodiversity

Neurodiversity is a science-based concept that people with learning differences have unique neurological wiring that causes them to think, learn and process information in atypical ways and these differences should be embraced as assets rather than "fixable" deficits.

The term neurodiversity includes autism and other neurological conditions. Autistic individuals are neurodiverse. Those who aren't impacted by autism are neurotypical.

Autistic or Person With Autism

A central question in the autism community is whether to use person-first or disability-first language when referring to a neurodivergent person. Person-first language puts the person before the disability, i.e. a person with autism. Disability-first language puts the disability before the person, i.e. an autistic person.

Some might wonder why this is a big deal. The phrases sound the same. They appear to mean the same thing. But for many neurodivergent individuals, they represent two different ideas that go to the heart of how they think about their autism.

"Person with autism" can imply that autism is separate from an individual, like baggage that can be lost at the airport or a disease that can be eliminated with the right medication. Autism isn't like that. Autism is integral to who a person is — to how they think and function. Many neurodivergent people believe that disability-first language better reflects that understanding. To quote a self-advocate:

> *"To take the autism out of me would be to remove everything that makes me me, and replacing that with a neurotypical way of thinking would make me somebody else entirely."*

These materials use disability-first language to highlight the basic idea of neurodiversity – that genetic variations are intrinsic to a person's sense of self and these variations merit the same type of equal respect called for in other forms of diversity, such as gender or ethnicity.

As with the conventions used for gender identities (he/she/they), it is a good idea to ask an employee whether they prefer person-first or disability-first in references to their disability status.

Non-apparent, Hidden, or Invisible Disability

The word "disability" may invoke images of building ramps, low-positioned drinking fountains, grab bars and other structural accommodations. But in many cases, autism isn't readily seen and doesn't fit our usual idea of what a disability looks like. Different terms are often used to describe less observable disabilities such as autism. Each carries a slightly different connotation.

Non-apparent disability is a neutral term which implies that a disability isn't easily seen.

Invisible disability is a term that suggests a person's disability can't be seen. This is similar to non-apparent disability, but some neurodivergent individuals give it a negative connotation, possibly because it may suggest a dismissive attitude about the disability.

Hidden disability is a term that may suggest a person is purposefully withholding information about a disability – actively hiding it as opposed to choosing not to disclose. Some neurodivergent individuals mask or suppress specific neurodivergent behaviors to match social expectations or gain acceptance. Masking is most likely used by individuals who are aware of social stigma, have experienced social rejection, identify as female or are working toward a specific goal, such as getting a job or fitting in with co-workers.

High-functioning Autism or Asperger's Syndrome

For many years, Asperger's Syndrome was a diagnosis given to individuals with non-apparent neurodivergent challenges in communication, sensory processing and executive function. Then in 2013, writers of the manual that doctors and clinicians use to diagnose mental/emotional disabilities reorganized the categories of autism-related disorders. Asperger's Syndrome was removed from the diagnostic list and all iterations of autism were lumped into the single category of Autism Spectrum Disorder with three corresponding levels of severity.

- Level 1 is the mildest form of autism *("requiring support.")*

- Level 2 is a slightly more severe form *("requiring substantial support.")*

- Level 3 is the most severe form *("requires very substantial support.")*

Some speculate that the diagnosis categories were changed because providers worried about the potential for "over-diagnosing" autism. The concern arose as autism prevalence in the United States was surging from 1-in-150 children in 2000 to 1-in-54 in 2016. Many providers believed diagnosticians were over-diagnosing autism by using Asperger's to signify "milder" forms of autism and avoid the stigma attached to the autism label. The change appears to have had little effect in that regard since prevalence has continued to grow from 1-in-44 children in 2018 to 1-in-31 in 2025.

Whatever the reason for the change, it complicates how individuals describe their autism to service professionals and the wider community. Many continue to self-identify as having Asperger's Syndrome to communicate the idea that they're "just a little autistic" rather than "really autistic."

Stimming

Each person works on a daily basis to stay regulated – to keep their brains and bodies calm and on task. Neurotypical people often stay regulated by using repetitive behaviors such as clicking their pen or tapping their foot or by engaging in comforting activities such as eating or going on a walk when they need a break. Autistics can find it especially hard to keep a sense of equilibrium and sometimes engage in repetitive behaviors called stimming (short for self-stimulatory behavior) which they find soothing. The frequency and appearance of stimming is different for each person. Some stimming is barely noticeable and some – such as rocking, flapping hands or using headphones – is easy to see. If you see an employee starting to engage in stimming behavior, it's probably a sign that they need a break or a self-soothing accommodation to restore their sense of calm.

Developmental Disability, NOT Mental Illness

Autism is a developmental disability and not a mental illness. There is confusion on this, partly because autism is generally diagnosed according to criteria in the manual of psychiatric conditions. Its inclusion in the psychiatric manual is an interesting bit of autism history. Autism was originally thought to be an emotional disturbance – a mental illness – but later was shown through research to be a developmental disability rooted in brain development. Our understanding of autism has changed, but the manual continues to include it as a diagnostic category. That said, many neurodivergent individuals do have overlapping mental health issues, such as generalized anxiety and depression.

What's the Difference?

A mental illness can include mood, anxiety and psychotic disorders and is often the result of external factors, such as abuse, trauma or long-term stress. Employees with mental health issues may have extreme mood changes or periods when they're unable to concentrate. Mental illness can be managed or go into remission with medication and psychotherapy and there is disagreement about whether or not mental illness is a lifelong condition.

A developmental disability such as autism is a difference in brain wiring that impacts how a person learns. This means they may be challenged when managing new situations. Unlike others who intuitively use context to guide them through changes, neurodivergent individuals need instruction to work out the appropriate and expected responses when circumstances don't fit their expectations. Autism is a lifelong condition with challenges that can improve with instruction in social and emotion management skills, but can't be cured with medication.

Why Does it Matter?

Making the distinction between a mental illness and a developmental disability is an exercise in thinking about why an employee may respond to situations in unexpected ways. This, in turn, helps ensure that employees get the type of support they need to function well in the job.

Accommodations for employees with mental illness and employees with developmental disabilities are similar. They may include reducing distractions in the work area, making changes in the sensory environment or using a flexible and supportive management style that includes more frequent meetings to help prioritize tasks. However, because employees with developmental disabilities have a unique system for processing information, job accommodations should especially focus on strategies that facilitate learning, such as using several forms of communication aligned with the employee's preferred learning style (written, verbal, charts or pictures) or using "to-do" lists and step-by-step checklists for tasks.

Key Points

- DEIA widens the talent search to ensure a business is hiring the best candidates. It's not about prioritizing one group over another.

- Neurodiversity is a viewpoint that atypical brain wiring in some people may cause them to experience the world in different ways. These differences are assets, not deficits.

- Autism is a difference in how someone learns. It is not a mental illness. It is best managed when employees understand the "whys" behind the behaviors of neurodivergent co-workers.

- Demonstrating your awareness of language nuances such as autistic person vs. person with autism can help you build rapport with neurodivergent employees.

A Different Operating System

Autism is hard-wired into brain functions at the root level and is likely the result of overcrowded pathways between different regions of the brain. This overcrowding impacts how neurodivergent people learn, solve problems and navigate a constantly changing world. Many people think neurodivergent individuals don't function well in "normal" situations. This is an incomplete picture at best. While neurodivergent individuals have processing errors when measured by neurotypical yardsticks – social awkwardness, sensory challenges and easy overload – many have positive attributes that are missing in the neurotypical population. It's a matter of being different, not less.

One way to understand neurodivergent differences is to compare the workings of the human brain to software systems that drive how computers process information. Let's say that the brains of neurotypical people run on a Microsoft Windows operating system. Autism isn't an app that can simply be installed or uninstalled on the Microsoft Windows system. Autism is a different system of its own – either Macintosh or Linux.

In this context, neither operating system is better than the other. Each has software that the other one doesn't. Each is more efficient in completing certain tasks than the other.

Challenges do arise when the different systems try to communicate (open each other's files). Linux has apps that try to open Microsoft Windows files, but Microsoft Windows doesn't have an app allowing users to open files from non-Windows systems. This is similar to how neurodivergent individuals experience a world in which they're a minority. The onus is on them to make themselves understood – to adapt their ways of doing things to match the expectations of the neurotypical community. They can do this with some success. But it comes at a physical and emotional cost that is exhausting and not sustainable.

The Autism Diagnosis Tic List

Autism is commonly diagnosed by psychologists or specialized doctors who use behavioral criteria published in the Diagnostic and Statistical Manual (DSM-5-TR). The DSM-5-TR uses two general categories with seven subcategories of different behaviors to make an autism diagnosis. This is a streamlined list of the behaviors from the Manual.

Communication (some challenges in all three)

- Reciprocity

- Nonverbal Communication

- Relationships

Repetitive Behavior Patterns (some challenges in two of four)

- Semi-voluntary repetitive movements (stimming)

- High need for sameness

- Strong interests in specific topics or objects

- Extreme over/under sensitivity to sensory input

7 Things to Know about Autism

Any account of autism can rapidly slip down a rabbit hole into a confusing pile of details. This section drills down to the essentials about autism with a focus on need-to-know information for those who supervise and work with neurodivergent individuals.

1) Each neurodivergent person is an "original"

Autism is called a "spectrum" disorder because it occurs in an infinite number of variations. No two people experience autism in the same way. Each neurodivergent person you meet will have different traits, personalities and communication styles from neurodivergent people you've met before. As noted by many in the autism community – "when you've seen one person with autism, you've seen one person with autism."

2) Autism is rooted in brain wiring

Researchers conclude that autism may result from anomalous brain wiring. At birth, an infant's brain is wired with 100 million brain cells – enough to meet every possible contingency. As the infant learns to navigate his new world, the brain fine tunes itself, discarding unnecessary neural connections and strengthening the useful ones in a process called pruning. The result is a narrowed and more efficient system for processing information.

With autism, researchers believe the pruning process gets stalled, leaving behind an oversupply of neural connections. When too many connections fire at once, an autistic person will likely experience an overload of noise and details and will find it difficult to muster a fine-tuned response appropriate to the situation. It's a neurological traffic jam that has few of the navigational signs needed to sort incoming information.

3) The spectrum is a circle

Many find it useful to sort differences in neurodivergent individuals by their level of skill, from high functioning to low functioning. The manual for diagnosing autism uses this framework, as does a graphic image commonly used as a symbol for autism – a multi-color flat line.

However, this high skill/low skill framework doesn't articulate what a manager should reasonably expect when asking autistic employees to perform workplace tasks. It implies that an autistic's skill proficiencies and deficits are fixed in all situations, omitting the fact that their skill levels are variable and may change in different situations. In conversations, an autistic employee may speak calmly when talking with co-workers, but sound anxious and stiff when talking to a customer. They may learn to perform a task in one context and find it difficult to transfer similar skills to a different context.

Rather than a multi-color flat line, autism is more like a wheel with colors representing different skill sets and varying levels of mastery within each skill set. Skill proficiency may vary from day to day and context to context, just as the skills of neurotypicals may be good, bad or meh, depending on the circumstances at the time.

4) Autistics are bottom-up thinkers

When getting new information, bottom-up thinkers take in details first, before broader concepts. Conversely, top-down thinkers take in concepts before details.

Most autistic individuals are bottom-up thinkers. Details are their informational currency. They take in information through multiple channels, which turns into a tangle of details they need to sort through before understanding what's being shared with them. This all takes place before they can decide how to respond in a conversation, or how to handle changes happening in their environment. As a result, autistic individuals have trouble "generalizing" or transferring concepts to different situations.

Neurotypicals, on the other hand, filter information and fill in gaps with general ideas based on past experience or established understanding. They're more likely to take something as given and then seek information to support it.

In the workplace, an autistic employee will likely need to understand the specific steps to complete a task before feeling confident enough to start it. Neurotypicals are more likely to jump in, focused on getting a job done and less concerned about how to go about doing it.

That said, autistic individuals are capable of conceptual thinking. It's just that they do it differently. They form concepts through a process of using information from different experiences to make connections among details and not through an immediate intuitive response. They need to understand tasks and the purpose of those tasks first. They question assumptions and don't tend to take things at face value.

For example, one employer tried to explain to an employee how to do a task by telling him, "Some people do it this way, I do it a different way. You should do it the way it works for you."

This approach is more confusing than helpful. A better option would be to list one set of steps for completing the task and stopping at that point. As the employee gets more familiar with the task, they'll find a routine that works for them.

5) Autistics' skills are spiky

Everyone has strengths and weaknesses. Neurodivergent people likewise have strengths and weaknesses, but their skill disparities are far more pronounced than those experienced by neurotypicals. They can excel in performing high-order tasks but fall short when asked to perform simple, basic skills that many would assume they could do given their high-order abilities. This can make it easy to misconstrue their skills across a range of tasks. A manager may notice that a new hire has a keen aptitude for one part of the job, so they add more work while withdrawing support they believe isn't needed.

This can create unrealistic expectations that will come crashing down when the employee asks a "simple" question which the manager assumes the employee shouldn't need to ask because they must already have the answer. Or the opposite may happen. A new employee may need support to train on one aspect of the job, so the manager overlooks them when assigning another task because they assume the employee won't be able to handle it.

When making these assumptions over the long term, the neurodivergent employee will feel stuck and will believe they won't have opportunities to stretch or grow in the company. On the company side, a manager may feel duped when an employee performs in a wildly different manner than expected. The bottom line is that these types of misunderstandings can be avoided if a manager gets to know the employee as an individual. Plus, believe a neurodiverse employee when they tell you what's easy and what's challenging for them, even if it's different from the norm.

6) Autistics take your words literally

Language has two layers of meaning: what words actually mean (their literal meaning) and what they're intended to mean (their figurative meaning). Autistics are literal thinkers who focus on physical objects and immediate experiences in their communications. When someone says one thing intending to mean something different (figurative meaning), there's miscommunication when one conversant doesn't intuitively understand the implied meaning. The best practice is to use precise, explicit language when speaking with neurodivergent people.

Example:

Jack: Did you see the logo I designed for our group?

Adam: Yes, I saw it. *[end of conversation]*

Adam answered the question. But Jack asked a question he didn't really want the answer to. He didn't want to know if Adam had seen the logo. He wanted to know whether Adam liked it or not.

Subtext

Autistics may find conversation subtexts confusing, but they can learn to understand their underlying intent and the expected response if they hear them regularly. With prompting and practice, Adam from the above example will eventually understand that he's expected to offer an opinion when someone simply asks "Have you seen … ?"

They're often quick to understand the intent of more direct statements or questions that prompt a specific action such as "Can you close the window?" – as opposed to "Please close the window."

Cliches

Autistics say cliches are easy to understand because they're used in everyday language, and everyone knows what they're supposed to mean. In other words, cliches are relegated to the ranks of non-figurative language.

Sarcasm

Autistics find it difficult to detect sarcasm unless it's used in an obviously negative or condescending way. Autistics can be coached to detect sarcasm by observing when a person's words don't match their tone of voice and/or nonverbal actions. Yeah. Right.

Metaphors, Analogies

Metaphors and analogies compare two unrelated ideas – one that is known and one that is unknown – as a way to explain an unfamiliar idea or to describe something in a novel or interesting way. Autistics often struggle to understand metaphors and analogies, possibly because they're hardwired to search for differences among details and ignore any similarities or comparisons.

7) Autistic senses don't always make sense

Sometimes we're in a place where things seem noisy, smelly or visually off-putting, but our responses aren't intense enough to profoundly impact our lives. This isn't true for many autistics, who can become easily overwhelmed by sensory stimuli because their brains aren't filtering sensory information in the "usual way." At work, they may be sensitive to loud sounds, bright overhead lights, people talking nearby as they're trying to work or the smell of a co-worker's lunch. Their sensory discomfort can make it hard for them to concentrate.

They may also experience challenges with interoception – the sensory system that perceives and interprets important body signals connected to their emotions. Interoception works by sending signals from the body to the brain, where they're interpreted as fear, pain, thirst, the urge to use the bathroom and other sensations or emotions. For example, if you notice that your mouth is dry, your brain interprets the sensation of dryness as thirst. If your stomach growls, your brain interprets the growling as hunger. Once you recognize thirst or hunger, you act on it by eating or drinking so the feeling goes away.

Interoception also affects how a person identifies emotions. Different emotional states trigger different sensations inside the body, which are then decoded to help us understand how we're feeling. An individual with weak interoceptive awareness will find it difficult to recognize their emotions because they can't make the connection between their body sensations and the emotions that trigger those sensations.

This lack of awareness of the sensory-emotion connection may lead a neurodivergent person to become dysregulated, which means they are losing their ability to cope with emotions such as stress, anxiety or frustration. Each individual manages their emotions in different ways, but there may be some clear indicators that an individual is having a hard time regulating their emotions, such as stimming, which – as noted above – are behaviors intended to promote self-soothing.

The Business of Disclosure

Many Autistics Don't Disclose

The question of disclosing an autism diagnosis is tricky for both autistics and employers. For autistics, the best answer often rests on the employer's level of understanding of autism, something an autistic individual doesn't typically know when applying for or starting a job. For employers, disclosure may raise concerns about how an employee's autism might impact other employees and their delegation of workloads.

For this guide, autistic individuals were asked questions about their job experiences and their decisions about disclosure. Each individual was asked whether they'd disclosed their diagnosis to any of their employers and their reasons for deciding whether or not to disclose.

Aside from those who worked in autism-related jobs – where being neurodivergent was a clear advantage – most said they didn't disclose because they were concerned about the consequences of disclosing. One individual said he doesn't disclose because he worries about how others might see him, especially the employer who might think his autism means he's not qualified for the job. Another said when he disclosed, his employer responded that they'd "try to be patient [with him]." Another individual said he thinks he's too high functioning to need help, but then described a situation when he'd missed learning about a change in procedure that a coach may have helped him learn in a more timely way.

However, one individual says she discloses because she has no interest in working for an employer that doesn't want to work with autistics.

These responses reflect the views shared with me by dozens of autistic adults during my years of work as an employment consultant and job coach. They also align with academic research on disclosure which concludes that autistics commonly believe disclosure is a risky step that is likely to trigger a negative response from an employer that might jeopardize their success in the job. It's just easier – at least in the short term – to stay silent on the matter.

Many Autistics Aren't Diagnosed

Autism is diagnosed with professional assessments of an individual's (generally a child's) behavior and developmental history. There isn't a blood test that can be universally deployed to diagnose each autistic individual, either in childhood or as an adult. A sizable percentage of autistics don't have a formal diagnosis and some self-diagnose as autistic.

The number of undiagnosed individuals is especially high among females and people with Black and Hispanic ethnicities. Females may be diagnosed less often - not because fewer are actually neurodiverse - but because females are often socialized in a way that makes any introverted tendencies and unusual interests seem consistent with social norms for their gender. Shyness in females is generally not considered noteworthy. Shyness in males is a diagnostic flag. Also, Black and Hispanic individuals are less likely to be diagnosed with autism than white individuals. These disparities are likely the result of socioeconomic or other barriers that translate to reduced access to evaluation and diagnostic services.

Bottom line: a company with a culture of support for neurodiversity is clearly helpful for employees who are diagnosed as neurodivergent. It is also helpful for employees who aren't diagnosed or who may not know they're neurodivergent.

Masking

Many autistic employees who choose non-disclosure may mask their autistic traits when they're on the job. They learn and mimic neurotypical behaviors to fit in with the company culture. Initially, employee masking may boost operational efficiencies for the company, but it has significant long-term costs for the employees' mental health, escalating their anxiety and depression and increasing their likelihood of early burnout. For employers, it often leads to high turnover among neurodivergent employees. This scenario reinforces the false, unhelpful narrative that autistic individuals are incapable of sticking with a job and successfully maintaining long-term employment.

Psychological Safety

Psychological safety in the workplace is how a person views the consequences of taking a risk when faced with the possibility of being seen as ignorant, incompetent or disruptive by co-workers. In a workplace with low psychological safety, neurodivergent employees are likely to choose nondisclosure and mask neurodivergent behaviors to fit in with the perceived expectations of co-workers. In a workplace with high psychological safety, employees feel confident that no one will embarrass or punish them for disclosing their autism and asking for help. They can focus on performing well in the job, which boosts their efficiency, job satisfaction and commitment to the company.

Many employers express their support for building a neurodiverse workplace, but may find it challenging to follow through when making adjustments in management styles to help neurodivergent employees feel psychologically safe enough to thrive in employment for a long period. In an Intel/ADP survey, HR professionals say they feel comfortable building their neurodivergent employees' trust and professional growth, but are skeptical about taking the steps necessary to help them feel safe, saying it's not their responsibility or it might cause conflict with their employer.

Building a psychologically safe culture requires a shift in management perspective – from a focus on accommodating the needs of neurodivergent employees to understanding that neurodivergent individuals are a critical part of the company who add value to the company's work because of their different ways of thinking. Autistic employees are a "culture add" if not always a "culture fit." They're highly capable and they add a unique point of view to the workplace. Not to mention … there's a clear benefit for neurotypical staff. Managers who work with neurodivergent people become better all-around managers as they improve key management skills such as giving feedback and setting clear expectations.

True INclusion

In a company where neurodivergent employees feel psychologically safe, it's important to not just hire a diverse team, but to also build a genuinely inclusive company culture where neurodivergent employees are integral to the company's success. Diversity and inclusion – ideas often used in tandem – are not the same. A company can hire a diverse team of employees, but not be an inclusive employer. Diversity is actively recruiting and hiring neurodiverse individuals. Inclusion is ensuring that diverse individuals are a valued part of the company. Diversity is a milestone while inclusion is an ongoing practice.

An inclusive company puts a high value on understanding different perspectives and making them a central part of organizational decisions. It's a workplace where neurodivergent employees know they'll be both supported and challenged in all aspects of work. They're less anxious about negative repercussions related to their autism and more confident in their ability to do the job well and in line with performance expectations.

Universal Design

Universal Design (UD) is an inclusive practice that companies use to make operational systems welcoming and usable to a widely diverse range of people. Just as good customer service means providing a welcoming environment, treating each customer with respect and giving them information they need, employees work best when they feel welcome and respected and receive adequate and timely information to do their jobs.

There are clear examples of UD in everyday life – curb cuts on streets and ramps to building entrances – that improve mobility for the different needs of people using wheelchairs, pushing strollers and riding bicycles. In the workplace, using UD to support various styles of learning may involve re-thinking procedures related to presenting information and managing expectations about performance.

Examples of UD at work include the consistent use of clear and concise language when giving instructions and outlining performance expectations. These are some general guidelines on giving instructions which can benefit all employees, whether neurodiverse or neurotypical.

- Use both oral and written instructions

- Give instructions in steps

- Cover one topic at a time

- Let employees take notes

- Allow time for employees to ask clarifying questions

- If possible, don't interrupt an employee with new instructions while they're performing a task

- Regularly review goals for tasks and job performance

Other UD practices can include offering remote work options to give employees flexibility in designing their workspace and managing their schedules. Managers can also re-think the formats they use for staff meetings, possibly opting for small, individual check-in opportunities as opposed to large meetings that require all employees to be at the same place at the same time.

A 3-Part Inclusion Blueprint

Building an inclusive workplace requires the use of three key strategies: visible leader advocacy; neurodiversity awareness training for employees; and operational flexibility. These strategies are based on overarching management principles that can be modified to fit the specific needs of different types and sizes of business. The strategies listed here apply to all types and sizes of companies, although some differ slightly for small and micro companies that operate under relatively informal management systems.

Leader Advocacy

Medium and Large Business

Leaders in medium and large companies set the course for their company's corporate values. Employees look to their leaders to get a sense of the company's commitment – or lack of commitment – to its stated priorities. An inclusive workplace will flourish when company leaders believe inclusion is linked to success and they take steps to initiate inclusivity reforms in company policies around recruiting, hiring, retention and promotion.

Small and Micro Business

In small businesses, the principals show a commitment to inclusion by leading with empathy. They actively listen to co-worker insights about workplace procedures or conditions. When issues arise, they focus on solving the problem rather than making judgments. If job performance is an issue, they talk with the co-worker privately about strategies to improve their work. Modeling empathy in these ways can help create a culture of mutual respect and respect for different ways of thinking.

Neurodiversity Awareness Training

Medium and Large Business

Front line leaders in large and medium companies influence company culture by deciding how to implement procedures that align with company priorities. Neurodiversity training for front line leaders is key to building an inclusive workplace where the neurodiverse perspective is taken into account and built into the systems for working with and managing employees. Training should be ongoing – continuously offered to reinforce employee understanding of neurodiverse thinking styles and approaches to solving problems.

Small and Micro Business

Neurodiversity training for employees of small and micro companies can be tailored to focus on core concepts like understanding divergent styles of thinking, promoting the use of inclusive language and defining practical strategies for communicating with neurodivergent co-workers. Training schedules may need to be flexible and can be offered via specialized online courses and regular short programs.

Operational Flexibility

Medium and Large Business

Inclusion strategies should be embedded in all aspects of company management - as you build your brand, recruit and onboard neurodiverse talent, and develop systems to monitor performance.

Managers can improve neurodivergent employee performance by giving extra thought to their communication strategies and management procedures. They can structure the workday, offer concrete ideas about how to perform job assignments, use a standard procedure for asking questions and offer consistent feedback, especially positive feedback.

Small and Micro Business

These strategies may also generally apply to small and microbusinesses, but will be less formal, especially with respect to the use of a standard procedure for asking questions. That said, offering consistent feedback is especially important for all types and sizes of business, because neurodivergent individuals are most comfortable when they know - with a clear sense of certainty - that they're correctly performing an assigned task.

Smaller companies that champion diversity may quickly experience a positive impact on customer traffic. Customers often prefer to engage with businesses that demonstrate a commitment to diversity and inclusion. Truly inclusive companies benefit from a word of mouth boost that translates to a positive reputation in their communities, which is important for smaller companies that don't have large marketing and advertising budgets. Small companies have the ability to build and sustain inclusive cultures swiftly and feel these benefits more quickly.

From Recruitment to Exit: Action Steps Across the Employee Life Cycle

Strategies to build an inclusive company culture should be a key part of human resource management as you build your brand, recruit and onboard talent, and develop systems to monitor performance.

Build Your Neurodiversity Brand

- Highlight the presence of neurodiversity champions within the organization.

- Leverage social media channels to highlight the company's inclusive culture.

- On the company website, feature a landing page expressly for disabled and neurodiverse individuals with concrete information on procedures for seeking accommodations and the availability of internal resource groups such as Employee Resource Groups (ERG.)

- Publicize neurodiversity support practices through professional associations, trade organizations, job fairs, business publications or anywhere job seekers may look for career opportunities.

Recruit Neurodiverse Talent

Talent Search

There are few direct pipelines where company recruiters can find neurodiverse job candidates or where neurodiverse job seekers can find inclusive companies with viable job opportunities. An effective recruitment strategy needs to be creative, multi-faceted and should include reaching out to educational institutions and service providers with strong connections to neurodiverse consumers. Organizations with access to neurodiverse jobseekers may include:

- Community and technical colleges

- Four-year colleges and universities

- State vocational rehabilitation agencies

- Private providers of autism support services

- Autism networks or trade associations (state autism societies)

Write Inclusive Job Postings

Highlight the company's inclusive work environment in job postings.

Work Environment

To promote an inclusive work environment, include in the job posting:

- Corporate values statement.

- How to ask for reasonable accommodations in applications and/or interviews.

Essential Duties and Responsibilities

Use plain language to describe the essential duties and requirements of the job in concrete terms.

General Rule:
Use words that aren't open to multiple interpretations.

Why?
Bottom up thinking style makes it difficult for neurodivergent candidates to understand broadly stated job requirements.

Use:
- High attention to detail.
- Interest in repetitive tasks.
- Oral/written communication skills.
- Job training and mentoring is included.

Don't Use:
- Excellent communication skills.
- Good team player.
- Ability to communicate with others.

General Rule:
Use simple, easy-to-understand format.

Why?
Bottom up thinking style and perfectionist tendencies.

Use:
Short lists of core job aspects – hours, salary, and essential skills.

Don't Use:
"Kitchen sink" lists.

General Rule:
Be clear that not all skills and qualifications are required.

Why?
Literal thinking – applicants may not apply because they think they must be highly proficient in every listed skill.

Use:
"or" between skill requirements

Don't Use:
"and" between skill requirements

Adjust Interview Formats

Inclusive workplace practices include making modest adjustments to interview formats and questions for job applicants with different backgrounds. To get the best possible information from neurodiverse applicants, hiring managers should take into account their bottom-up thinking style when framing interview questions.

Also – before any interview, it's a good idea to ask all job applicants if there is any information they want to share or any accommodations they want to request – without asking a specific question about their disability status. It may also be helpful to give potential employees a list of questions to think through prior to the interview. Top of mind thinking is not always easy for every neurodivergent person.

General Rule:
Consider interview location.

Why?
Possible sensory dysregulation.

Use:
Closed, quiet space to conduct interviews.

Don't Use:
Interview rooms with loud noises, bright lights.

General Rule:
Ask closed questions.

Why?
Bottom-up thinking – difficult for applicants to understand question with little / no context.

Use:
Closed questions – "Tell me about any jobs or volunteer work you've done in the last 5 years." "What tasks did you find most enjoyable?"

Don't Use:
Open questions – "Tell me about yourself." "Why do you want this job?"

General Rule:
Ask questions based on the candidate's real/past experiences.

Why?
Bottom-up thinking – applicants will quickly understand questions with specific context.

Use:

In any of your past jobs, did you do any filing or data input? What procedures did you use to do that?

Don't Use:

What did you do in your past jobs?

General Rule:

Don't use hypothetical or abstract questions.

Why?

Bottom-up thinking – difficult for applicants to understand question with little / no context.

Use:

Think back to a recent job. How did you feel when people interrupted you?

Don't Use:

How would you cope with working where there are lots of interruptions?

General Rule:

Ask about possible support needs for tasks which are part of essential job functions.

Why?

Bottom-up thinking – clarify job expectations while inviting applicant to think about support needed to succeed in job.

Use:

Ask applicant whether they can perform essential function tasks with or without reasonable accommodations.

Don't Use:

Are you capable of doing this job?

General Rule:
Tell the candidate if they are drifting off-topic in an answer.

Why?
They may find it hard to judge how much information you need.

Use:
Thank you, that's enough information. I'd like to ask you another question.

Don't Use:
Sharp cutoffs when they talk too much or start talking off-topic.

General Rule:
Prompt the candidate in order to gather sufficient and relevant information.

Why?
Candidate may find it hard to judge the type of information you need.

Use:
Would you like to share more information about the types of tasks you did in previous jobs?

Don't Use:
Do you have anything to add?

General Rule:
Avoid business jargon where possible.

Why?
Candidate may interpret your language in literal terms.

Use:
"Too many things to do."

Don't Use:
"Too many balls in the air" or "Too much on your plate.'"

General Rule:
Be aware that eye contact may be fleeting or prolonged.

Why?
Eye contact is a problematic communication skill for many neurodiverse individuals.

Use:
Patience!

Don't Use:
Coaching to "correct" eye contact habits.

General Rule:
Don't expect much small talk. If the candidate engages in small talk, expect that it may involve their unique interest.

Why?
Small talk is challenging for many neurodiverse individuals. When pressed to engage in small talk, they may revert to conversation about a subject they're comfortable with.

Use:
Patience!

Don't Use:
Chatter to fill silent moments.

General Rule:
Be patient if they take a while to answer a question.

Why?

Given their brain wiring complications, candidate may be relatively slow to understand what you're asking, especially in complex or hypothetical questions.

Use:

Words to assure the candidate they can take the time they need to answer a question.

Don't Use:

Words suggesting that candidate has a limited time to answer a question.

General Rule:

Describe the post-interview hiring process.

Why?

Neurodivergent individuals are less anxious when they understand what will happen next.

Use:

Description of next steps in hiring process, including approximate timeline.

Don't Use:

"We'll get back to you."

Take Time with Onboarding Procedures

Onboarding procedures are critical to helping neuro-diverse employees understand and fulfill their job functions. Training materials should be concise. Supplementing written materials with oral training can facilitate learning for neuro-diverse employees, who often take longer to process new information.

The process may take a little more time to ensure neurodiverse employees are ready to take on their work responsibilities, but the company will benefit in the long run. With a strong onboarding process, neurodiverse employees may need less hands-on management over time and will perform their assigned tasks at a higher level. They will be confident in their ability to perform and will have a high degree of job satisfaction, which means they will commit to the company for a long period. This reduces employee turnover which can cost at least 1.5 to 2 times the amount of an exiting employee's salary plus the hidden costs of advertising the position, training the new hire and recovering lost productivity.

Onboarding is the best time to demonstrate a key value of the company for new hires – that managers are willing to take time to understand the perspective of neurodivergent employees and to take that perspective into account in how they communicate and monitor their performance. That said, managers must also set and communicate clear boundaries about the ongoing limits of their availability so that attending to a neurodivergent employee's needs doesn't disrupt their overall duties and company-wide system requirements. As noted earlier, reciprocal understanding – managers understanding employees and employees understanding managers – is vital in a company with a thriving, inclusive culture.

It's commonly understood among HR professionals that successful onboarding relies on implementing "The Four C's:" compliance; clarification; culture; and connection. They can be generally defined as follows.

- *Compliance* involves teaching a new employee the basic rules and policies of the organization, including how to complete required paperwork.

- *Clarification* requires ensuring that a new employee understands their roles and responsibilities.

- *Culture* means teaching a new employee the norms for the organization.

- *Connection* means helping a new employee build relationships with co-workers and facilitating their sense of value to the team.

Culture and connection go hand-in-hand. They are the trickiest of the four C's, but they are critically important when onboarding neurodiverse employees who may have challenges with communication and deciphering context.

Cultivate an Inclusive Culture

Some key elements of a company culture you might share with a new employee are:

- How the company treats employees

  - Is there an employee recognition program?

  - Does the company host all-staff social events?

- The company's mission

  - Do employees have a shared sense of purpose?

- Company norms for making decisions

  - Do managers ask for employee feedback or are decisions made unilaterally?

- How people communicate with each other

- Does the company have an open or "keep-to-yourself" style of communication?

- Company expectations around work style and volume

  - Is the atmosphere laid-back or high-performance?

  - Do employees have flexibility around where and when they work?

  - Does the company support work-life balance or are employees expected to respond during off-hours?

Foster Co-Worker Connection

Neurodiverse employees may initially be reluctant to participate in company-sponsored relationship building activities. Awareness of supportive company programs – like those listed below – may help neurodiverse employees view the company as a psychologically safe place, mitigating their anxiety about the perceived risk of "putting themselves out there" with co-workers:

- The availability of multiple internal channels to disclose (employee assistance programs, HR, direct manager, intranet portal)

- Enterprise-wide neurodiversity training programs

- The use of neurodiversity understanding as an indicator of excellence in employee performance reviews

- The existence of Employee Resource Groups

- The availability of formal mental wellness programs and policies

Mentoring programs – which pair experienced employees with newer employees – can be an especially effective tool to help neurodivergent employees reduce their frustrations when they need to review company expectations or ask questions about how to perform tasks. One of the neurodivergent individuals interviewed for this Guide was emphatic that working with a mentor made the critical difference in jobs where she was successful.

There are three key strategies for mentors developing a successful mentor/mentee relationship with neurodivergent employees:

- Establish trust and comfort from the start so mentees feel comfortable sharing their challenges and asking questions they might otherwise be afraid to ask.

- Understand common mentorship topics, such as organizational and time management techniques, managing deadlines and breaking down and prioritizing tasks. On interpersonal issues, mentees might ask for guidance on workplace communication, including understanding expectations, communicating their needs, and resolving misunderstandings with co-workers.

- Share your experiences to help employees gain insights about resilience, motivation and personal growth.

Beyond those types of programs, neurodivergent employees may need an additional nudge to work on building relationships with their co-workers. It may also be useful to invite them into shared employee activities or leverage technology to foster co-worker communication. Note, however, that it's also important to make sure they understand that participating in co-worker opportunities are optional and not required. Ideas for co-worker participation opportunities may include:

- Offering participation in company joint committees

- Offering participation in community volunteer or social projects outside of work

- Holding monthly coffee/lunch chats within or across departments

- Communicating event-related days to all employees such as national "name it" days, birthdays or work anniversaries

Provide Clear, Consistent Communication

Managing employees requires a delicate balance of guiding them through missteps while also encouraging their continued good work. This is true for managing all staff, whether neurodivergent or neurotypical. But it may be uncharted terrain for managers who are new to working with a neurodivergent employee.

As noted in another section of this Guide, a key to managing neurodiverse employees is to think beyond their in-the-moment behaviors and remember the "whys" that drive their approach to their work tasks and co-worker communications. That doesn't mean managers need to stray from the company's policy on performance expectations. Rather, the challenge is to continually communicate – provide them with concrete and actionable feedback on a consistent and predictable basis.

Chunking Information

Chunking information is a useful strategy for communicating with all employees, but especially with those who are neurodiverse. Chunking involves breaking tasks into small, manageable "chunks" and can be applied in training, project management and daily task management.

Training and Onboarding

- Teach skills in short modules, such as a 15 minute video on one topic and followed by practice.

Project Management

- Divide projects into clear, small tasks.

Task Management

- Dedicate blocks of time to small tasks, such as "Email Hour" or "Task Performance Block." This can reduce distractions and context switching.

Communication

- Present key points in short lists (5-7 items).

- Use short paragraphs.

- Start new sections with titles.

Change Management

- Break down large organizational changes into small, achievable steps.

Informal Feedback by Employer

Because neurodiverse individuals work best in situations with a high level of predictability, it's helpful – ideally as part of the onboarding process – to spend time with them outlining company procedures for both giving ad hoc feedback and conducting performance reviews. This is true even if the information is included in an employee handbook. It's also beneficial to talk with them about the definition of feedback, which is neutral information – not personal – about how someone is performing a task. When actually giving feedback, it's helpful to begin and end with positive comments about the employee's overall performance.

It is not always obvious to a neurotypical person why a neurodiverse employee is struggling or making errors. Ask them. In a diplomatic manner. Direct communication is the best approach for working with a neurodiverse employee. Also be open to a new way of doing a task. A benefit of hiring neurodivergent people is their unique way of being. Rigid thinking is a two-way street.

Informal Feedback by Neurodivergent Employee

When neurodivergent employees give feedback to co-workers or managers, they can be characteristically direct and honest. Diplomacy isn't their strong suit. This communication style may come across to others as intentionally rude or mean, but invariably, that's not the case. In fact, a neurodivergent person would likely be upset to know that others thought they were being rude. A job coach can work with the employee on their tone and delivery or co-workers can learn about neurodiverse communication styles and accept them for who they are.

Giving Instructions

When giving instructions, it can be useful to include details about how to complete a task. For example, it's not sufficient to simply tell a neurodivergent employee they need to complete their task by its deadline. This may cause confusion and needless anxiety, because, given their bottom-up style of learning, they may not intuitively know how to break the project down into small, manageable steps to meet the goal. It's best to take a few minutes to go over the steps required to complete the task – without going into excessive detail. Examples of how to simplify instructions are included in the section on Universal Design.

Performance Reviews

Job performance feedback for neurodiverse employees should be offered in a concrete and nonjudgmental way and should focus on key areas of success and areas for improvement on job goals agreed to at the start of employment. Feedback should be brief and should focus on specific tasks the employee has completed. For example, simply telling an employee they've done a good job is likely too vague and doesn't give them anything tangible to build on. A more constructive approach would be to say "I liked what you did when you … "

The same applies to negative feedback. Instead of saying, "You did it wrong," offer information about what to do differently. Employees should also be given an opportunity to ask clarifying questions. As with all other employment phases, using ambiguous language or unclear directions can easily cause an employee to be confused about what is expected of them.

Key Points

- Think about neurodiverse learning styles.

- Consistently communicate with neurodiverse employees.

- Patience pays dividends in employee retention.

- Enjoy the employee's contribution to the company.

What Autistics Say

Six neurodiverse adults - mid-20 years old to early-30 years old - answered questions about their experiences in the workplace. They shared thoughts on what did – or didn't – help them be successful in the jobs they've held. They also talked about their decisions regarding disclosure and what they want employers to know about how to best work with neurodiverse employees.

Note: Just one of these individuals is female. That is not an accident. Far more males than females are diagnosed with autism, possibly because social standards and expectations for females are different than they are for males. A female who is shy or who has intense interests (think unicorns) is often considered within "normal" expectations for their gender. A male who is shy or who has intense interests is more likely to generate questions that lead to a diagnosis.

Jean

> *"Be open to new approaches and assume good intent."*

Types of jobs she's held

- Direct Service Provider and Personal Care Attendant for people with developmental disabilities

- County Case Manager for people with developmental disabilities

- Data Analyst

- IT Director

Jean works remotely as an IT Director for a data collection and analysis company. Before working in tech, she worked as a case manager and direct service provider for counties and a private organization. One of her most positive job experiences was working for a county social service agency in the Pacific Northwest where she had a mentor for her first six months of employment. She now lives in the Upper Midwest, where she has held similar disability support jobs - one for a county government and one for a private disability support organization - before transitioning to work as an IT professional.

What helped her be successful

- Mentorship! At both of her favorite jobs, Jean had an assigned mentor from day one. She was expected to meet with the mentor daily at first, then weekly as she got settled in. The mentor was a safe person she could approach with any and all questions.

- A smooth onboarding process with time to gain a clear understanding of what she is expected to learn along with a timeline.

- Clear, consistent expectations and instructions – not minute by minute scheduling.

- Clear feedback and communication.

- A welcoming, nonjudgmental community.

- Doing work she is passionate about and interested in.

- Working in a sensory friendly environment.

- Working for a company that fosters a creative problem solving attitude.

At her job in the Pacific Northwest, colleagues and managers were genuinely accepting of all people. They didn't infantalize employees and everyone had jobs tailored to their strengths.

Employees were encouraged to make the environment work for them. It was never a hindrance to ask for something you needed to make your job better - Dragon Speak, assistive tech, individualized lighting in each office. Employees didn't need doctors' notes to seek an accommodation and it was expected that if a person was asking for something, they know themselves best and should receive that support.

As an IT Director working remotely, Jean can work a flexible schedule and her home already fits her needs. She says "the people make a huge difference." Her managers and co-workers are very welcoming. They aren't as aware of disabilities as at other places she's worked. Everyone is included in work events and social gatherings and there is no negative talk about other employees. Also, there is a great online culture where employees get to know each other via video meetings (Zoom), huddles (Slack voice/video) or in fun and random channels like #random, #toons-and-grooves, #PETS and #data-dumps.

What were her main challenges?

Jean's key challenges in the workplace have been:

- Bad sensory environment.

- Co-workers/management talking negatively or infantilizing people with disabilities.

- Inconsistent leadership and expectations.

- Inflexible thinking and problem solving attitudes.

- Passive communication.

- DEIA trainings.

Disclose?

Jean disclosed to her employers and has *#ActuallyAutistic* on her LinkedIn profile. Many have suggested she remove this tag because it might cause implicit bias. But she says she has no interest in working for an employer that doesn't want to work with autistic folks. She understands this sounds like a privileged approach, but it's worked for her. She has a job she likes and has positive relationships with people in her industry.

Jean's message for employers...

If you're going to do a DEIA training, have people with lived experience teach or co-teach the training. "Nothing about us without us."

Most DEIA trainings about disabilities are simply offensive and outdated. Also, pay the people teaching and don't expect them to volunteer their time and energy to teach others.

Make accommodations the norm, not something special you need a doctor's note for.

Be open to new approaches. Many autistic people have a great ability to see reality - this means seeing all of the inefficiencies, and unnecessary social niceties that get in the way of having a clear and efficient approach to the job.

It's helpful to discuss social structure and expectations. This might be taboo, but it's super helpful. Is it expected if someone does something to help you out that you also help them? Is it uncouth to ask certain questions? How do you interact with people below, at your level and above you in the organization's structure? When is it OK to say no or to draw boundaries?

Assume good intent. Be curious! Ask what they meant in a non-confrontational way.

Andrew

"I only need minor accommodations."

Types of jobs he held

- Education services
- Sports management and logistics

Andrew works as a paraprofessional in a classroom for autistic students at a local high school. In off hours, he's a site coordinator and team liaison with the school's sports teams. In off-off hours, he's behind the wheel of his car as an Uber and Lyft driver. Before working as a paraprofessional, he assisted sports teams at the state college where he earned a four-year degree.

Andrew's dream has been to own his own home. He worked hard at his Uber and Lyft jobs to save money for a down payment on a house. He successfully earned enough money from those jobs to achieve his goal of buying a home despite the objections of mortgage lenders who are highly skeptical of "gig income" as a source of reliable financial support.

What helped him be successful

Andrew says he has a sense of belonging in both his classroom and sports team jobs at the high school. His classroom co-workers understand autism and he doesn't have to use extra energy to mask his autistic behaviors. Classroom co-workers also rely on him to re-direct students when their behaviors become disruptive and their reliance on him gives him confidence about his role at the school and his ability to perform well in his job. Overall, school leaders promote a culture of understanding and they encourage collaboration among employees. He cites the culture of understanding and his co-workers' confidence in his abilities as the key contributors to his success in these jobs.

What were his main challenges

Andrew's toughest challenges occurred in his job as an assistant to college athletic teams. He said those jobs promoted intense competition among team players and staff, noting "There's one way to do things correctly and if you don't do it that way, you're out." In this environment, he continually used masking to fit in. He said the effort was exhausting and it undermined his energy and confidence in his ability to support the team.

Disclose?

Andrew disclosed his autism to supervisors and co-workers for the school jobs, because his autism was a clear advantage in his work supporting autistic high schoolers. However, he didn't disclose to his supervisor on the sports team in college, because he knew he'd be judged differently in an environment that demanded high levels of conformity and speed.

Andrew's message for employers ...

> *"I'm not less than a neurotypical person. I'm just wired differently and I process things differently. I can be successful and I'm determined to learn. I just need some minor accommodations to help me succeed."*

Dan

> *"I need concrete information and constructive feedback."*

Types of jobs he held

- Sorting mail, data entry (work study at four-year college)

- Nursing home aide

- Paraprofessional in charter school for autistic secondary students

Dan held several work study jobs while he was a student at a four-year private college. Since graduation, he's held jobs in the human and social services sector. Two of those jobs involved providing services to autistic youth – as a camp counselor and a paraprofessional at a charter school for autistic secondary school students. He's also worked as an aide at a group home for individuals with Hungtington's and other disabilities. Dan loves performing in theatrical productions and does voiceover gigs.

What helped him be successful

Dan says he feels as though he's not been successful in the workplace so far. His most positive experience has been working as a camp counselor with autistic youth, where supervisors and co-workers understand his perspective.

What were his main challenges

Dan says he was frustrated in the work study mailroom and data entry jobs because he received little instruction on how to do the required tasks and frequently had to ask for directions. When he disclosed his autism, his manager replied that they'd "try to be patient with [him]." He was laid off from that job.

His most frustrating experience was working at the group home, which he described as "an intense juggling act" that involved continual multi-tasking. He had little training and his performance expectations weren't clear. His instructions for task assignments were complicated and confusing – "Some people do it this way, I do it a different way. You should do it the way it works for you." The feedback he received was judgmental and not constructive and generally consisted of a statement like "you did it wrong" with little information about what he should do differently.

Disclose?

Dan disclosed his autism at his work study jobs, but chose not to disclose at the group home. In the jobs in which he worked with autistic youth, his autism was common knowledge among co-workers and supervisors and he didn't disclose in the formal sense.

Dan's message for employers ...

Dan's suggestions for employers are: communicate often and clearly; provide opportunities to get to know co-workers; and exercise patience when giving new information. More specifically, he'd like employers to use direct and concise instructions, ask neurodivergent employees what they need to be successful in the job, provide visual images to support instructions, hold regular staff meetings and offer opportunities to get to know co-workers. Regarding performance expectations, he wants employers to know each neurodivergent person is unique, neurodivergents often move at a slower pace (they're not lazy) and they may be somewhat vague in their communications, especially at the start of a new job or task.

Greg

"I need a reliable company contact and different formats to communicate work tasks."

Types of jobs he held

- Test engineer (contract job/on-site)
- Software engineer (contract job/remote)

What helped him be successful

Greg says he prefers working on-site where it's relatively easy to find help when questions arise. In onboarding for the test engineer job – an on-site position – his supervisor gave him an industry book to read and left him alone for a week. He said he didn't feel productive or useful that week. After the "reading week," he met members of his team, attended industry subject matter lectures and performed simulation tests. He officially joined the team when he successfully completed the simulations.

Of the onboarding tasks – reading, listening to lectures and running simulations – Greg found the simulations most helpful because he was doing something concrete, not simply listening to someone explain things.

For the software engineer job, Greg said that initially, all the instructions he received were verbal. He asked to also get instructions in writing and the company gave him written instructions, which he found helpful.

What were his main challenges

Greg described onboarding for the software engineer job – a remote position – as "chaotic" largely because of inconsistent messages given by the recruiter and the contract company and because he didn't have a consistent point of contact when he wasn't sure what to do. Days and even weeks went by when he didn't get anything done because he was lost and didn't know what to do and didn't have anyone available to answer his questions. A month into the job, he had a one-day notice that his supervisor was leaving the company. The supervisor was the only person he knew and he "worked" for a week without a manager.

Disclose?

Greg hasn't disclosed because it's hard to do and he doesn't think he needs to. He said he doesn't think there's a stigma attached to disclosing, but he worries that his employer might think he's not qualified for the job or he might need a lot of extra help or would view him as being different from other employees.

Greg's message for employers ...

Greg stressed the importance of consistent communication and support, especially during the onboarding process. It's important to have a reliable point of contact who is easy to reach. Also, supplementing oral instructions with written instructions is helpful in ensuring full understanding of tasks and the employer's expectations.

Colin

"I need employers to understand my autism and give me individual tasks to focus on."

Types of jobs he held

- Grocery store (assistant manager; cashier)
- Movie theater

What helped him be successful

Colin works full-time as an assistant night manager at a grocery store and part-time (10 hours/week) as a concessionaire and ticket taker at a movie theater. He worked the day shift at the grocery store for eight years and was recently put on the night shift (10 p.m. to 6 a.m). He performs a wide variety of tasks. He rotates and faces products, operates the cash register, watches the self-checkout machines and helps department staff with deliveries. He says he is most comfortable and attentive when he can work without interruption and when there's a manager or co-worker available to deal with problems.

He feels calmer and more productive at the movie theater job because "when something goes wrong, someone else takes care of it." The grocery store job, on the other hand, "goes into hyperactive mode when it gets busy" and he's continually interrupted. He prefers the night shift because the pace is relatively constant and there aren't many interruptions.

What were his main challenges

Colin's main challenges are multi-tasking (doing regular checkout while also keeping an eye on self-checkout lanes) and transitions (abruptly moving from the back end of the store to the front end and cashiering). He also gets confused when he's asked to perform tasks outside his written job description.

Disclose?

Colin has disclosed to both of his employers. At the grocery store, he has a job coach who works with his boss to figure out workplace adjustments that are feasible for both Colin and his employer. An example – Colin's schedule was moved to the night shift when the customer flow is slower and there are fewer interruptions.

Colin's message for employers ...

Companies should learn more about autism and how it impacts people. I am hyper-focused and I obsess about things. My focus makes me more efficient and less lazy. I do best when I can focus on

*one thing at a time. When I'm asked
to multi-task, I get overwhelmed and
sometimes go into sensory overload.*

Tristan

*"I need employers to put instructions in
different formats and explain why they
change procedures."*

Types of jobs he held

- Customer service - fast food and concessions

- Warehouse - product recycling

- Product retrieval for customers

What helped him be successful

Tristan worked for seven years in the warehouse of a pharmaceutical company, where he rotated expired medicines and assisted with the delivery of products. He currently works for a furniture and home goods retailer, retrieving products for in-store and online customers. Like Colin, he believes he performs best when he can work without interruption. He prefers a predictable schedule, which he had at the pharmaceutical company, but has adapted to a scheduling system in his current job that varies from day to day and week to week.

What were his main challenges

Tristan's main challenge is processing information dumps when new instructions or procedures are introduced. He feels anxious when his work flow is interrupted by co-workers or frustrated customers. He also is sometimes unclear about the reasons for changes in some procedures and he'd like to know more about the "whys" behind those changes.

Disclose?

Tristan didn't directly disclose to the pharmaceutical company, but the company was aware of his diagnosis. He didn't disclose his diagnosis to his current employer.

Tristan's message for employers ...

> *It would be helpful for important information to be communicated to employees in different formats. Please remember that "it's a spectrum, not one size fits all." Also, it would be helpful to know that you understand how we "work" because we process information differently.*

Questions Asked of the Six Individuals

- Please list the jobs you've had leading up to where you are now. If you've had a lot of jobs, just list the ones you've had for the longest period of time.

- Which job was your most positive workplace experience? (You can list more than one)

- What helped you be successful in that job?

Examples:

  - Predictable hours

  - Friendly manager

  - Clear, understandable tasks

  - I could take breaks when I needed to

- What was challenging in that job / those jobs?

Examples:

  - Unpredictable hours

  - Little or no feedback about my job performance

  - Confusing task assignments

- Sensory overload – noise, lighting

- Did you disclose your autism diagnosis to any of your employers?

- What do you want employers to know about you?

- Do you have comments or ideas you'd like to share?

Final Takeaways

Building a truly inclusive company isn't about prioritizing certain employees. It doesn't mean a company has to compromise on performance standards or make changes in employee job functions. An inclusive company culture ensures the success of neurodivergent employees while sharpening the management and customer service skills of the entire workplace staff. It also has a positive impact on how the company is perceived by the larger community.

Neurodiversity is the idea that no two brains work in exactly the same way. Each person is differently abled and is celebrated for their individual skills and assets, not dismissed because of their differences. The term "neurotypical" describes someone who processes information in ways that are typical in their culture. The term "neurodivergent" describes someone who processes information in ways that diverge from cultural norms. Autistic people are among those who identify as neurodivergent.

Autistic individuals make positive contributions to a company where they're truly included in a workplace culture that values reciprocal understanding of employer and employee differences. They thrive when managers and co-workers think about why they act in unexpected ways and then use that understanding to inform their managerial responses in positive, productive ways.

Many autistics don't disclose their diagnosis and a sizable percentage don't have diagnoses with official documentation. A company with a culture of support for neurodiversity can be helpful for all employees, whether neurotypical or neurodivergent – diagnosed and undiagnosed.

Resources

Some of these resources focus on workplace skill training for neurodiverse employees. While workplace training for neurodiverse employees is important, the focus of this Guide is the other side of the equation – identifying strategies to improve employer understanding of how their neurodiverse employees approach new tasks and solve problems.

Note: we have no affiliation with any of the organizations listed here. All links were valid at the time of publication.

Autism at Work Playbook

University of Washington Information School.

https://bpb-us-e1.wpmucdn.com/sites.uw.edu/dist/c/19989/files/2024/04/AutismatWork_Playbook2021-a7df2592425eace2.pdf

Unmasking the System: Toward Sustainable and Inclusive Employment for Autistic Adults

Ali Raja

https://www.preprints.org/manuscript/202506.0893

"Becoming an Autism-Informed Organization" Series

Autism Society of America

https://autismsociety.myabsorb.com/#/course-bundles/a4f1d0c1-b686-4bdc-a9fa-51e9e5dd8957

Hire Autism

Organization for Autism Research

Free on-demand online training for employers, including modules on inclusive hiring and coworking.

https://www.hireautism.org/

Win for Employers

Autism Speaks

https://www.autismspeaks.org/win-employers

AIM - Autism Internet Modules

The Employee With Autism

https://autisminternetmodules.org/m/1041

About the Author

What I know about autism is what I've learned from my adult neurodivergent son plus 15 years of coaching scores of neurodivergent young adults as they navigated the transition from parents-home-school to independent living. I'm an attorney and teacher by training and while I've sometimes used my professional degrees for their usual purpose, my work with neurodivergent adults has called on my legal and love-of-language skills in unexpected and rewarding ways.

I've worked with neurodivergent students as a teacher, job coach, job search consultant and post-secondary navigator. I've written lessons in self-advocacy and social competence for neurodivergent youth and adults. I've co-produced social skill learning videos that are used by teachers throughout the U.S. Most recently, I co-founded an organization called Spectrum Connections, which provided coaching services to neurodivergent job seekers in Minnesota and Wisconsin.

This Guide is the result of that work which focused on supporting neurodivergent adults as they endeavored to fit the mold of their employers. It highlights the idea that neurodivergent success in the workplace is a two-way street which requires reciprocal understanding of the "why" behind management procedures and employee behaviors.